Riding the Waves

Contents

Chapter 1 — We're Off! ... 4

Chapter 2 — Sun, Sea, and Sand Dunes ... 10

Chapter 3 — Making a Splash ... 19

Chapter 4 — Jellyfish and Lemon Ice ... 23

Chapter 5 — Surf's Up! ... 27

Anthony McGowan
Illustrated by Jon Stuart

Steck Vaughn®
HOUGHTON MIFFLIN HARCOURT
Supplemental Publishers

www.SteckVaughn.com
800-531-5015

Property of Cypress Christian School Elementary

In this story . . .

Max

Jet

Jet's mom

Jet's dad

Toby
(Jet's brother)

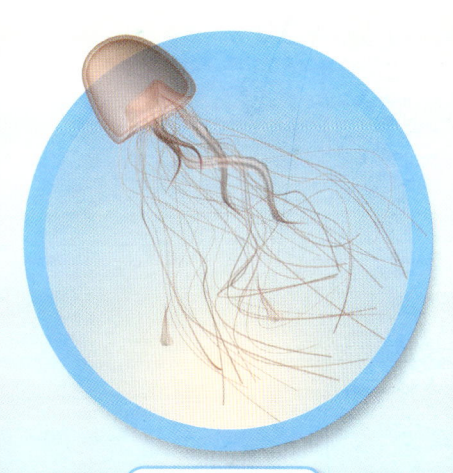

Jellyfish

Chapter 1 — We're Off!

"OK everyone, time to go!" said Dad, opening the car door.

"Seatbelts on," said Mom.

Jet and his family were going to the beach for a week. Jet had been doing well at school, so he was allowed to bring one friend. It was a hard choice, but in the end he picked Max.

It was a long drive to the beach. Toby and Jet argued all the way. They argued about what music to listen to. They argued about what games to play. They argued about whose turn it was to read the comic book.

Finally, they reached the campsite.

"Where's the water?" asked Toby.

"Not far," smiled Mom. "It's a nice walk to the beach."

"Let's put the tents up and then go take a look. The exercise will do us all some good," said Dad.

It took them forever to put up the tents. Toby had to share a big tent with his mom and dad. Max and Jet had a tent all to themselves.

Toby was jealous that Max and Jet had their own tent. He pulled their tent pegs out and the tent collapsed.

Ha! Ha!

Max and Jet put up their tent …again!
"We'll see you down at the beach," said Mom. "If you just follow the path, you can't get lost."

"Toby is so annoying," grumbled Jet.

Max pulled out something from deep down in his backpack.

"This might cheer you up," he said.

"You brought the micro-buggy!" exclaimed Jet. "Let's take a ride."

Chapter 2 – Sun, Sea, and Sand Dunes

Max and Jet turned the dials on their watches and …

Then they climbed into the micro-buggy and sped off across the sand dunes.

In no time at all Max and Jet were at the beach. They even got there before Mom, Dad, and Toby.

They grew back to normal size and waited for the others to arrive.

"How did you…?" said Toby, puzzled.

"Shortcut," said Jet, grinning.

"Look at this," said Max, pointing at a poster for a surfing competition.

Kids' Surfing Competition!

This Friday

First prize: a new surfboard

Second prize: a mask and snorkel

Third prize: a bucket and spade

Sign up in the Coral Cove Gift Shop

"Let's try and win!" said Jet, excitedly.

"You'll never be able to learn to surf in a week," scoffed Toby. "I had lessons last year. I was the best in my group."

"Why don't we all try it," said Dad, cheerfully.

They rented wetsuits from a shop on the beach, but the shop only had one surfboard left. They took turns using it.

Toby *was* very good. He didn't fall off, not even once.

Dad was terrible. He couldn't even stand up on the board.

Jet found it very hard, too. He managed to stay on his feet for a few seconds but then he fell off.

"I said you'd be no good," Toby sneered.

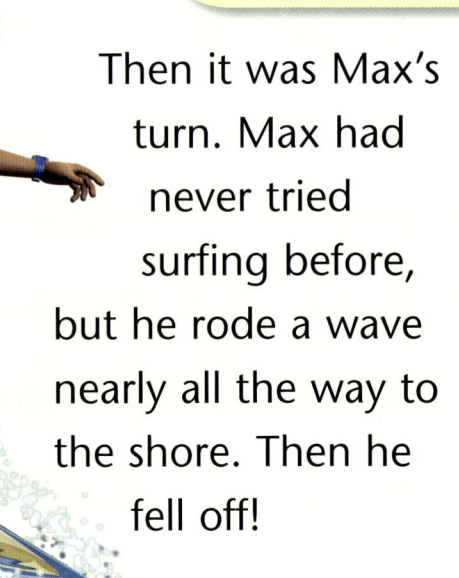

Then it was Max's turn. Max had never tried surfing before, but he rode a wave nearly all the way to the shore. Then he fell off!

"I'm going to win that competition," Toby boasted. He grabbed the surfboard.

"Hey! Share that with your brother and Max!" ordered Dad.

But Toby was already strutting up the beach to join the older children.

"We have to beat him," said Jet.

"I don't see how we can," Max replied. "Unless we practice."

"Cheer up, you two," said Mom. She handed Max and Jet a lemon-ice cup and a wooden spoon each.

They had been so busy thinking about how they could beat Toby that they hadn't noticed Mom slip away.

Max finished his lemon-ice. He scraped the last bit out of the cup. Then he stared at the wooden spoon.

"Jet, I have an idea," he grinned.

Chapter 3 – Making a Splash

Early the next day, they all headed off to the beach. Max carried the micro-buggy and Jet put the lemon-ice spoons in his pocket.

"Where are you going?" asked Toby.

"Just to play with our toy car," said Max.

"How fun," Toby sneered, "little toys for little boys. I'm going to hang out with the surfers."

Out of sight, Jet and Max changed into their wetsuits. Then they used their watches to shrink. It was Jet's turn to drive the buggy. He went full speed, bouncing over the sand dunes and shells.

They found a rocky part at the edge of the shore. There was no one else around.

"There," said Max, pointing at a large rock pool. "We can practice without anyone watching us."

They practiced all morning, surfing the small waves in the rock pool. Once, a crab came out to watch. Jet fell off his board with a splash, scaring the crab away.

"I'll never be able to do this," he moaned.

"Don't give up," said Max, "You'll get the hang of it."

Chapter 4 – Jellyfish and Lemon Ice

Jet and Max practiced surfing every day. They found bigger rock pools, with scarier waves. They watched out for each other to make sure they were always safe.

Max was getting really good. He could do all kinds of tricks. Jet was getting better, too.

Sometimes the micro-surfboards broke. The children didn't mind – it just meant that they had to eat more lemon-ice!

The day before the competition, they had one last practice session. This time they didn't practice in the shelter of a rock pool. They found a quiet part of the beach and practiced in the ocean.

As they finished riding their first wave, Max saw something gleaming in the water.

"Oh, no," he cried. "A jellyfish! Let's get out of here!"

The boys had to surf for their lives. They just managed to escape the stinging jellyfish.

When they were safe on the sand, Max said, "That was the best you've ever surfed!"

Chapter 5 – Surf's Up!

It was the day of the competition. The beach was crowded. A man with a megaphone called each person's name. Some of the competitors weren't very good. That cheered Jet up a bit.

"At least I won't be the worst," he said.

"NEXT TO SURF," called out the man with the megaphone, "IS TOBY."

Toby splashed into the water and got up on his board. He did two amazing stunts. The crowd shouted loudly – even Jet had to cheer.

Then Toby tried to do a handstand on the board. He got it wrong and fell into the ocean. Poor Toby came out of the water looking disappointed.

Next it was Max's turn. He did some neat tricks. Jet whooped and cheered.

Then it was Jet's turn. When his name was called, he paddled out, but he was too nervous to surf back. The water gleamed. Then, to his horror, he saw why. There was a jellyfish!

Jet jumped up onto his board just as an enormous white-tipped wave picked him up. Soon Jet stopped thinking about his nerves or the jellyfish. He was enjoying the ride way too much.

Before he knew what was happening, he'd reached the beach.

"That was fun!" he said.

The time came for the winner to be announced. It was Jet! Mom, Dad, and Max all rushed up and congratulated him.

"I knew you could do it!" said Max.

"How did you learn so fast?" asked Dad.

"With the help of jelly and lemon-ice," grinned Jet.

I had to let him win. He is my little brother, after all!